WORKING TO

The Co-operative Concept

Co-operation is — working together.
Pat Bolger is author of the definitive work on the Irish
Co-operative Movement and he lectures on co-
operation at the University of Ulster. In 1982 he was
awarded the highest honour of the Irish Co-operative
Movement — the Plunkett award for co-operative
endeavour.

WORKING TOGETHER

The Co-operative Concept

PAT BOLGER

THE O'BRIEN PRESS
DUBLIN

First published 1985 by
The O'Brien Press Ltd.,
20 Victoria Road, Rathgar, Dublin 6.

British Library Cataloguing in Publication
Data
Bolger, Pat
Working together: the cooperative concept.
1. Cooperation — Great Britain — History
I. Title
334'.0941   HD3485.A4
ISBN 0-86278-089-6

Printed in the Republic of Ireland

The author acknowledges the co-operation of the
Electricity Supply Board in the publication of this book.

CONTENTS

CO-OPERATION IS ...

Co-operation simply means working together.

When we work together, helping each other even at the most trivial task, we are *co-operating.*

Co-operation has been defined as 'the basic social process'. It is the simple concept of two or more people working together for a common aim, and as such Co-operation is as old as mankind. You could call it the *method* of all constructive human activity. Without co-operation we could not have *exchange* which is the basis of all *business.* Business depends on the exchange of goods for goods, goods for services, goods and services for money and so on.

Co-operation can be *formal* or *informal;* and indeed it can be *conscious* or *unconscious.*

Informal co-operation is where we help each other in a casual unplanned way — for example, we come across somebody who needs help to lift a heavy object, to push a motor car or to drive livestock. Neighbours have an unspoken agreement to help each other as the need arises. Workers often choose to come together informally to work in pairs or small groups rather than working alone. Digging can sometimes be a tiresome and monotonous job if everyone works alone in his own garden. Helping each other we usually get all the gardens dug more quickly — and we ourselves have more fun!

Enjoying each other's company when working together is the *social* advantage of Co-operation. Getting the work done better and more quickly is the *economic* advantage.

Formal co-operation involves planning beforehand and organising the activity and perhaps also sharing the equipment, materials and the different tasks. A simple example might be that of a number of men owning and working a fishing boat.

Formal co-operation is usually undertaken because there is a *felt need* for it. There is something to be done (even a risk to be shared) which is beyond the power of the single individual to do at all, or to do without great difficulty or expense. It may be done better, more quickly, more safely or more profitably if a number of people are involved. Can you think of examples of each case?

Formal co-operation involves formal agreement on the part of the co-operators, a set of rules and regulations, and often a system of rewards and penalties.

The international postal system is a good example of formal co-operation.

In rural Ireland we still have the old system of co-operation known as the Meitheal in which neighbours sometimes come together to help each other in sharing the farm work, to plant and harvest their crops. This Co-operation is partly *formal* and to a great extent informal.

We have said that co-operation can be *conscious* or *unconscious*. *Conscious* co-operation really explains itself — it is where the co-operators all *know* each other, they see and understand *why* they are working together.

On the other hand the girl picking tea-leaves in a tea plantation in India or Sri Lanka is really co-operating with many people to provide me with a cup of tea. There is the farmer who owns the land, his workers, the packers, the railwaymen, the shippers and sailors, the wholesaler and the shopkeeper. Without them I could not get my cup of tea or get it so easily. Yet each of them does his own part without being very *conscious* or aware of the others. Very few of them know each other and, what is very important as we shall see, is that the whole activity is not always undertaken for the benefit of all the co-operators. It is possible that some of them may be poorly paid for their work and that the user may have to pay too much for the tea.

Localised co-operation is more likely to be a conscious effort whereas co-operation which involves a wide geographic spread or a great number of people is more likely to have a certain amount of *unconscious* participation.

Co-operation is often classified under the headings 'indigenous' and 'institutional'.

INDIGENOUS CO-OPERATION

Indigenous co-operation simply means the forms of exchange, helping and sharing which grow up naturally in the lives of people. In the first instance these forms of mutual help were necessary for survival. They were shaped to fit the needs of the people in the community for working and living. In turn, these patterns of co-operation once they were set up, helped to shape the lives of the people — their business, their social life, their customs and their culture. Indigenous co-operation is an on-going thing. There are always changes taking place, so the indigenous co-operation in every society is always changing and adapting itself to new situations as people's lifestyles evolve and change. The rural Meitheal which used to be one of neighbours co-operating to build large haystacks is now likely to be made up of a smaller number of farmers sharing tractors and machinery in the making of silage. In every new urban housing estate we can see patterns of indigenous co-operation taking shape as the new residents come together to develop ways of mutual help to meet their individual and collective needs. These can vary from simple arrangements between neighbours as to cooking, shopping and child minding to more organised systems for recreation and the provision of useful services.

INSTITUTIONALISED CO-OPERATION

Institutionalised Co-operation describes what is generally known as the Co-operative Movement — a very special type of formal Co-operation which has a very definite design and a customary set of rules and regulations. With some changes from country to country, this same design and same set of rules (often called Co-operative Principles or Co-operative Guidelines) are accepted all over the world. 'Institutionalised' is perhaps not the best word to describe the Co-operative Movement. It is more helpful to think of it as Co-operation by Design. The Co-operative Movement does not seek to 'institutionalise' people, to regiment them or limit their freedom by rigid structures with endless rules and regulations. Rather it seeks to liberate them and give them real freedom in control of their own affairs. It is a free, voluntary, conscious Movement of people working together for a good and useful purpose. Every Movement has to have an Ideal. The ideal of Co-operativism (The Co-operative Movement) consists in taking what is the basic method of working together (co-operation) and putting it to work in such a way that everybody who takes part and does his fair share will benefit fairly and equitably from it.

THE CO-OPERATIVE MOVEMENT

It is nowadays generally agreed that the Co-operative Movement, as we know it, had its origins in the little cotton town of Rochdale in Lancashire, England. The popular legend has it that 'twenty eight poor weavers of Rochdale often out of work, out of money, and sometimes short of food' came together saving a few pennies each week until they had a capital of £1 each which they used to open a small grocery shop (the Toad Lane store) on the shortest day of the year (21st December) in 1844. This in itself was nothing unusual. It is known that by that time there were over 250 such groups of workers in various parts of Britain doing something similar. This was the time of the Industrial Revolution and there are horrifying stories of how workers, including women and young children were treated under the new factory system in the "dark satanic mills" of industrial Britain. The workers had to work cruelly long hours in bad conditions for very low wages. They were poorly housed, poorly fed and in some cases were urged at their tasks by "rude language, threats and blows". Also in many cases, workers in order to keep their jobs were bound to feel obliged to buy their groceries and household goods in the

A group of the original Rochdale Pioneers.

shop owned by the factory foreman or mill owner. There were also some shopkeepers who cheated their customers by over-charging, giving short measure, charging an unfair rate of interest on bills and often adulterating the produce. Common examples of adulteration were the mixing of white china clay in household flour and the adding of dried spent tea-leaves to good tea.

This small band of workers in Rochdale formed themselves into a co-operative society called the Rochdale Equitable Pioneer Society. History books frequently refer to the founder members as the Rochdale Pioneers. They had much wider aims than the mere running of a successful grocers shop. They hoped to start a movement which in time would reform the whole order of society — a system wherein greed would be replaced by generosity and concern for people, where nobody would grow rich by oppressing others, where labour would employ capital rather than capital exploit labour and where workers could enjoy the benefits of their labour. Some of the workers were dispossessed small farmers, labourers and rural craftsmen forced to seek work in the factory system. They valued their old sharing-and-caring rural way of life in the village community and felt that it should be possible through the savings of workers to set up a system of co-operative self-governing (and largely self-sufficient) communities combining the best aspects of the old and new methods of agriculture and industry — using the machines and inventions of modern times to create wealth and happiness instead of human misery. Co-operative communities would exchange their surplus products on the basis of their labour value. Children, old people, the sick and infirm would be provided for by a system of insurance and community care instead of having to endure the horrors of the poorhouse and the orphanage. The spread of co-operative communities would usher in the era of peace and plenty where there would be no wars, no grinding poverty, no greed, no exploitation or oppression — a New Moral World.

ROBERT OWEN

One of the great advocates of this co-operative approach to creating a 'New Moral World' (sometimes referred to as Utopian Socialism) was Welshman Robert Owen (1771-1858) a self-made millionaire industrialist, reformer and philanthropist. Robert Owen is often referred to as the Father of Co-operation because he had such a powerful influence on the development of the Co-operative Movement. He succeeded very well in business because he treated his workers as human equals, paid them well and provided for their education and general welfare. His factories were models of technical and business efficiency demonstrating the good effects of understanding and co-operation between workers and employer. Owen helped to found a number of co-operative communities or communes — in Britain, America, and a famous one in Ireland at Ralahine, Co. Clare. Few of these were very successful and the ones (like Ralahine) that were, did not last very long. The ideal was often not properly understood and it was very hard for such a movement to make progress because people's minds were not attuned to the idea of co-operation. The harshness of their lives moved them more to 'compete' and to take advantage of each other for personal gain.

Other famous men who were associated with Owen in advancing the idea of co-operation and self-help included Dr. William King of Brighton, William Thompson of Cork and John Doherty, a Donegal man who was one of the founder fathers of the Trade Union movement in Britain. In those days the twin movements of co-operativism and trade unionism worked very closely together.

What made the Rochdale Pioneers remarkable — and the reason why they are so well remembered — was the set of rules which they adopted for the running of their society. These rules later became known as the 'Rochdale Principles'. With certain small changes these same Rochdale Principles are the guidelines which govern the thinking and the conduct of Co-operative societies throughout the world to-day. The Rochdale 'Principles' or guidelines may be listed briefly as follows:

1. Open membership
2. Democratic control
3. Limited return on capital
4. Distribution of surplus in proportion to trade
5. Cash trading
6. Selling only pure unadulterated goods
7. Education of the members and the public
8. Political and religious neutrality.

Again we must understand here that the title of *Principles* is somewhat misleading. Strictly speaking there is *only one co-operative principle* and that consists in taking what is the *method* of all constructive human activity and putting it to work in a particular way to make a system of 'voluntary, conscious working together of people in an organised manner for a worthy common aim and where the product or benefit of the activity is shared equitably between all who take part'. Very simply, it involves taking the method and making a principle of it. What are commonly referred to as Co-operative Principles are really ways which have been found to make the core Co-operative Principle happen, and work well in practice.

Horace Plunkett (1854-1932)

Plunkett is generally acknowledged as the 'prime mover' in the foundation of the modern Co-operative Movement in Ireland in the 1890s. Guided by his inspiration the first co-operative creamery was established in Dromcolliher, Co. Limerick, and by 1910 there were over a thousand co-operatives of various kinds established throughout Ireland. He was also largely responsible for Ireland getting its own Department of Agriculture in 1899. (For further information see: Margaret Digby, *Horace Plunkett: An Anglo-American Irishman*, Oxford, Basil Blackwell, 1949, and R. A. Anderson, *With Horace Plunkett in Ireland*, London, Macmillan, 1935.)

OPEN MEMBERSHIP

A Co-operative society should normally allow any person to become a member. The applicant must, of course, be qualified and be prepared to accept the responsibilities of membership. A particular co-op may not always be able to accept everyone as a member, but if membership has to be restricted temporarily for good and prudent business reasons, this should be done fairly and without favour. Persons should not be excluded because of their race, class, language, culture, religion or political beliefs. The aim of the Co-operative Movement is to overcome the divisions which tend to make men enemies rather than brothers. Incidentally, it was the Co-operative Movement that first gave women equal rights with men in membership, share holdings, property-owning and voting, long before women were given any rights or entitlements in private business or public politics.

The idea behind the open membership 'principle' is that business should be done for the benefit of all who can work at it, and should not be confined and exploited to create riches for a few.

DEMOCRATIC CONTROL

In a Co-operative society the member is more important as a *person* than as a *shareholder.*

In ordinary commercial concerns such as partnerships and private or public companies, the shareholders are given voting rights according to the amount of money they have invested in the enterprise. Thus a person with a thousand shares will have ten times more voting power than one with only a hundred shares. So it is that if I own 51% of the shares of a limited company I have complete control and almost total power over the business of that company even though my ideas about running the business may be unacceptable to the other shareholders. In a Co-op the general rule is 'one man, one vote' regardless of shareholding.[1]

In *secondary* co-ops (e.g. where a number of trading co-ops come together form a wholesale society) voting powers are arranged at the start on a basis that is accepted as being democratic, reasonable and fair. The arrangement may take into consideration the number of members in each *primary* Co-op and the amount of trade it does with the secondary society, but the aim is to ensure that in any situation the strong do not overpower the weak and that *people* are never outvoted by *money.* The member with a single £1 share has as much say and as much voting power as the one with several

---

[1] Sometimes the rule is modified to allow extra votes to members with long and devoted service in the Co-op (usually to a maximum of five votes) but members are never given voting powers which would outweigh those of a majority of their fellow members.

thousand pounds in shares.

Just as the open membership 'principle' rejects the idea of the individual or small group cornering profitable business for exclusive private gain, the principle of democratic control also stresses the importance of *people* and rejects the concept of 'the divine right of Capital' which grew up at the time of the Industrial Revolution and which said that those who supplied the money or capital (the 'risk-takers') had the right to control the whole business, determine the policies, make all the decisions and even order the lives of other people — wage-earners, suppliers, service agents etc.

LIMITED RETURN ON CAPITAL

Some co-operative societies do not pay their members any interest on the share capital which they invest to start up and run the co-operative. The directors feel that the benefits and services (such as better prices or cheap credit) which the member gets from his membership of the Co-op are reward enough. They seek to focus people's minds on the *working* benefits of Co-operation, the advantages gained day and daily in a community that works together giving people more control of their own affairs and opening up opportunities for better business and better living in the future.

Others feel, however, that the Co-op should pay its members some direct return on the cash they have invested, comparable to what their money could have earned had they put it in a safe investment e.g. the bank or the post office.

Before they learn the full meaning of what Co-operation involves, people brought up in a capitalist tradition like to have an assurance that their money will earn something. The payment of a small (even tiny) dividend may be very helpful in raising member morale and providing some defence against scoffers who laugh at the co-operative idea and make jokes about 'investing money for nothing' .

In any event, the rate of interest paid to co-op shareholders is always low. Sometimes the interest rate allowed is given in the rules of the Society. Sometimes it is decided upon from year to year by the members at the annual general meeting.

The principle of limited return on capital is a reaction against what happened in former times e.g. during the Industrial Revolution when capitalist manufacturers and businessmen expected and made large returns on the capital employed in the business. Returns of 30 to 50 per cent were not uncommon and quite frequently the total cost of setting up a factory was recouped in the first year i.e. a return on capital of 100%.

Rev. T.A. Finlay S.J. (1846-1940)

Thomas Aloysius Finlay, Professor of Political Economy at University College Dublin, was one of Plunkett's ablest and staunchest supporters in the Co-operative Movement. As a student of German, from 1871 to 1873, he had made a detailed study of the Raiffeisan system of co-operative credit. He later set up the system in Ireland when the first co-operative credit society was established in Doneraile, Co. Cork, in 1894. These credit societies, or 'village banks', were very similar to the modern credit unions.

Such high rewards for capital could only be got at the expense of others and often caused great distress amongst primary producers of raw materials (farmers, miners), workers and consumers, when the market was manipulated by those who had control of money.

In most co-operative societies the sale of co-operative stock and shares is forbidden. They cannot be bought and sold on the market like the shares of capitalist private or public companies. The transfer of co-op shares from member to member or applicant member may be done with the consent of the management board of the society. Usually such transfers are only allowed to be transacted at par i.e. the face value of the share. Thus, there can be no trading or speculation and nobody can grow rich (at the expense of others) by dealing in co-op shares.

PROFIT OR 'SURPLUS'?

Co-operative societies normally serve their members by providing extra services and/or giving favourable prices on goods sold or produce bought. They are non-profit organisations in the sense that they do not make money through dealing in the same ways as private businesses or public companies.

However, the word 'profit' is sometimes used loosely in reference to co-ops financial accounts. What appears under the heading of profit in the trading account of a co-operative is quite different from the ordinary profit in private business. A co-op is a community of persons trading to provide themselves with goods or services at first cost so the 'profit' shown in accounts is really the surplus of members' money paid in, or, in other words, the difference between the estimated and the real cost.

People often find this distinction between profit and surplus difficult to comprehend. It may be best understood by a simple illustration from a 'primitive' example of co-operation. We take the case of seven housewives who come together as housewives often do to complain about the cost of groceries. They have reason to believe that if they combine together to purchase all their household requirements in bulk they can do better business. To simplify their initial experiment they draw up a list of items and quantities which they all use (over a longer or shorter period depending on the size of each household). Then they do a rough estimate of the likely cost of this common 'package' of goods and find that shopping individually at local shops the cost would be approximately £40. They are hoping that in bulk buying the cost may prove considerably less but they are not yet sure of this. So to be on the safe side and to avoid any embarrassment they put in £40 each and select one woman of their number to do all the buying. This buyer will be usually a person who has shown initiative and leadership qualities and who has a good knowledge of where the best prices can be got — an able dealer! She will, however, have certain expenses such as the cost of phone calls (to enquire about prices), travel, transport and perhaps delivery charges and tips before she has all the goods assembled and delivered home.

When the business experiment is completed we may find the financial picture something like this:

		£
7 Housewives contributed £40 each	—	280
Purchase of goods plus buying costs	—	245
		35

What does the figure of £35 above represent?

It is the surplus of the women's own money left over after the transaction. They are clearly not making money and will not be doing so. All they and their families will be doing is consuming e.g eating and drinking, washing, polishing etc. using up all the goods they have spent money on.

If, instead of keeping the goods themselves, the women sold the goods to their neighbours outside the group, for, say, a nett £273.

		£
Sale of goods	—	273
Cost of goods	—	245
PROFIT	—	28

This is an obvious profit because money has been made at someone else's expense. The fact that the seven women paid in £40 each at the start has nothing to do with it. At the end of the sale they have their own money (£240) plus £28.

If they kept and consumed the goods for themselves all they would have is a saving or 'surplus' — £35 of their own money!

With this £35 surplus a very obvious thing for the women to do would be to 'distribute the surplus' simply and fairly by taking back £5 each, and be quite satisfied that they had done good business in procuring for each member at a cost of £35 goods which in the ordinary way might have cost £40 or more — not to mention the cumulative expense and trouble of individual shopping.

On the other hand, they may reason that this £35 is money which in the ordinary way, shopping as individuals, they would not have. They decide to keep this money in reserve with a view to gradually saving and building up capital to do bigger things. They look into the prospects of expanding their bulk-buying experiment and find that with a larger number of housewives buying together they can further reduce their household costs. Co-operative shops often have their beginnings with a small number of people who start buying together in a small way, learning about the ways of business as they go along, taking others into the group, and really 'educating' themselves and their neighbours in the benefits of Co-operation by practical demonstration. They gain a great deal from their own experience; but from the start they can have advice, guidance and sometimes material help from established co-operatives and from the organisations which promote Co-operation.

CO-OP SHOP

We now look a few years ahead and see the situation that can develop from the humble start of a few neighbours working together.

We now have some 200 housewives who are buying their goods together. In order to be able to buy sufficient volume of goods at the right times to get the best prices they have seen the need for storage space so they have rented premises which they now operate as a neighbourhood Co-operative Shop. Here they assemble and distribute the goods and generally organise their business. Their organisation is now registered as a Co-operative Society with the Registrar of Friendly Societies. This affords the members certain protection and safeguards under the law.

To rent and pay the running costs of the shop, to build up adequate stocks of a variety of goods and to employ paid help, Capital is needed. This has been provided in a number of ways:—

(1) Each member has committed herself to contribute say £50 by way of share capital. This may be paid all at once or by instalments.

(2) Some money has been obtained by way of loan or overdraft from the Credit Union, commercial bank or other lending agency. The loans may have to be secured by the personal guarantees of a few individual members who are persons of means.

(3) Suppliers of goods provide some short-term credit e.g. goods supplied at the beginning of the month may not have to be paid for until the end of the month.

The position now is not quite so simple — particularly with regard to the pricing of goods. It would be difficult to know what would be the *precise cost* to the member of a particular item because—

- Goods are bought at different times from different sources in varying quantities and, therefore, at different prices
- Some goods have a quick turnover, i.e. they are taken up quickly by the members. Others lie in stock for varying lengths of time
- Transport and other direct costs may vary
- There are also other costs and overheads which must be allowed for but which would be impossible to divide and allocate to specific quantity/ items of goods — wages, heating and lighting, telephone, postage, wrapping materials, bank charges, etc. In a shop handling possibly a thousand different commodities and items with different turnover times it is hardly possible to determine the precise amount that these costs add to the overall cost of, say, a pound of tea.

If the members try to 'price' the goods too keenly there is a danger they may underestimate their costs. Some unexpected increase in wholesale prices or overheads could leave the shop making a loss. Members in a co-operative are not just like ordinary customers in a commercial store 'buying goods from the shop' even though to all external appearances they seem to be doing just that. What the Co-op members are doing is *supplying themselves* with goods and paying in an agreed amount of money for each item.

The members through their committee or board of management will agree on a pricing policy. Different approaches can be taken with regard to the amount of money members will be required to pay in for goods taken out, for example:

(i) Members may agree to pay prices somewhat less than those charged in ordinary commercial shops or supermarkets, but sufficient to ensure that there will be at least a small trading surplus.

(ii) Members may agree to pay prices which are the same as those in local shops. This usually ensures that a substantial surplus is shown at the end of a year's trading. This is a very sensible approach. The surplus can be distributed, or else re-invested to help the Co-op grow and develop. It also forestalls any claims of 'unfair competition' on the part of private vested interests and may help to avoid price wars or trade boycotts designed to break the Co-op.

(iii) In the ordinary way a Co-op will not budget to provide goods to its members at prices which would result in a financial deficit but there is nothing wrong with this if the members are all agreed to make good the deficit later on. It is basically a device whereby Co-op members, through their organisation, give themselves credit. It is, however, an

George William Russel (Æ) (1867-1935)
George Russell was born in Lurgan, Co. Armagh, but lived most of his life in Dublin where he was a leading figure in the Irish literary renaissance. In 1897 he joined Plunkett in the Co-operative Movement as organiser of co-operative credit banks in Connacht and Donegal. He published several volumes of poetry as well as his famous books *Co-operation and Nationality* (1912) and *The National Being* (1916). (Courtesy National Gallery of Ireland).

operation that is usually fraught with difficulties and dangers.

In a situation where there is an intense campaign of unfair competition designed to attract customer members away from their co-op and break the co-operative organisation it may be necessary (but hopefully only for a short period) to budget for a deficit. In such cases the trading loss is often underwritten by (a) a number of the co-op members (b) another co-op organisation (c) other supportive organisations or individuals.

In an ordinary private shop a customer goes in and buys goods for which he pays a *final* price. Having paid the money and taken the goods the transaction is finished and the customer has no further involvement or commitment.

In a Co-operative shop the member does not *buy* the goods — he owns the shop! The buying has already been done collectively by him and the other owners. When the member (part owner) takes goods from the shop he pays in what is in effect a 'payment on account' approximating to the real cost of the goods. Accurate accounts are kept and if at the end of the accounting period the 'payments on account' made by the membership amount to more than the total costs and expenses there is a trading 'surplus' — if less there is a deficit.

In either case this is the concern and responsibility of all the members.

DISPOSAL OF SURPLUS

The trading surplus is the members' own money. The co-operative principle/guideline lays down (and it is only commonsense) that all the members who have contributed to the surplus should have a say in what is done with that surplus. This is done at the annual general meeting. Depending on the rules of the society the first matter for decision may be whether or not they pay a dividend on share capital, and if so at what (limited) rate of interest.

The remaining surplus must then be disposed of. The alternatives are:

1. *The entire surplus may be voted to 'reserves'* to be used by the Co-operative as a whole to help it in its business. This is often done when (a) the surplus is very small (b) the Co-op, though making good progress, has still got sizeable liabilities (c) a period of less favourable trading is foreseen in the future (d) resources are needed for further expansion and development.

2. *The surplus may be distributed to the members*
    This distribution may be in cash or by way of additional shares allocated.

    Either way, the method of distribution is strictly laid down.

In a private company the profits are distributed in proportion to each person's *shareholding* in the company. In a Co-operative society this is not permitted. Distribution is done, not *in proportion to shareholding but in proportion to the amount of trade done by each member.*

Thus a member who has taken £1,000 worth of goods from the shop gets ten times more 'surplus' than the member whose trade was £100 — even though the latter may have twenty times more share capital invested in the Co-op.

This again makes good sense — the people who have taken most goods have paid in most money and by far the greater part of the surplus arises because of the money paid in excess of the true cost of the goods.

It is of course true that the member who has invested a lot of share capital also contributes something. Less share-capital might make it necessary for the society to have more loan capital. Interest charges are a cost which reduces the size of the surplus. Similarly a large share capital may make it possible to instal machinery and equipment in a layout which gives greater efficiency and productivity thus reducing costs and increasing the surplus.

The Co-operative idea, however, is that Capital gets its reward by way of a limited dividend on shares (Principle 3). It is felt that the dividend should be no more than is sufficient to maintain the value of the money invested, without making a large profit. There is a feeling too that particularly in the early days of their Co-operative effort and where their cash investment by way of share-capital is usually quite small, members should be prepared to forego any direct return — for the sake of the wider benefits which Co-operation brings.

It is not that co-operators fail to appreciate the importance of Capital but that they require something more! The great emphasis is on Involvement. Co-operation is a dynamic — an active working together which requires something more than the single act of investing money. The Co-op needs the members' *continuing* support and involvement — participation in co-operative business and co-operative organisation. This is why a member's trade is much more highly emphasised than his capital and why it is generally more highly regarded when surplus is distributed.

CASH TRADING

In the days of the Rochdale Pioneers cash trading was a strict rule; but more than that it was a dire necessity! The little Toad Lane store was very short of *working capital* which made it difficult to keep an adequate stock of groceries and to replace them as they were 'sold' to the members. Goods could only be given out for 'cash on the nail' because the Co-op got little or no credit from wholesalers and suppliers. The Rochdale co-operators made a very strict rule of no credit — and they stuck to it. Indeed there are some heart-rending stories of how they had to enforce the rule against each other — even where some of their founder members went hungry rather than make an exception of themselves.

Nowadays cash trading is no longer enjoined as a strict co-operative 'principle' — but it is still very strong in the co-operative mind. In the modern world most people could not live without some form of credit — in fact credit can be very useful and profitable if it is used for productive purposes or to reduce costs. Credit to stock a farm or equip a factory can result in much better productivity and higher profits. Credit to build one's own house may prove much cheaper than paying rent for a flat; credit to buy a bicycle may pay for itself quickly from the saving on bus fares!

Even in the matter of buying ordinary consumer goods people often find it annoying or time-consuming to have cash in hand at all times for every little purchase. It is frustrating to have to make a double journey home and back because one is a few pennies short of the price of an article. When a person establishes a reputation of credit-worthiness many shopkeepers are quite happy to do business with him as long as he settles his bill regularly at the end of the week or the end of the month as arranged.

Credit, however, presents great dangers for people who are un-disciplined and self-indulgent, and also for poor people beset with some domestic crisis e.g. parents may become quite reckless in pursuing possible cures for an incurable child. The Co-operative thinking enshrined in this co-operative principle was the encouragement of industry and thrift amongst co-op members. Members should have a spirit of sturdy independence — promptly and willingly paying their share in all financial commitments, both with their fellow co-operators and with others. The member of a trading co-op who is slow to pay and who continually seeks to drag out his credit is being unfair and unjust to other members particularly where the Co-op has to carry a large bank overdraft to provide this credit. Far from contributing to a trading surplus, he is reducing it!

A good Co-op, on the other hand, will always strive to do its business with maximum skill and efficiency and provide such a good service that its individual members will prosper, and so achieve a position of financial independence that they will be able to become 'cash customers' in practical terms.

The Co-operative Movement, however, has not confined itself to the negative approach to credit, as might be suggested by the 'cash trading' rule. Whilst deploring the lack of thrift and the hopeless unproductive debt into which people fall or are pushed, the Co-operative Movement has taken

Harold Barbour (1874-1938)

Barbour was the grandson of the founder of the great linen manufacturing firm of William Barbour of Lisburn, Co. Antrim. In 1897 as a successful young businessman, he was greatly attracted by the co-operative approach of Horace Plunkett. There followed forty years of quite remarkable service to the Co-operative Movement in every aspect of its organisational and business activity. A man of small stature who retained an extremely boyish appearance well into middle age, Barbour's lifestyle, and that of his wife, was characterised by outstanding generosity. He is generally agreed to have been the greatest of the great 'northern co-operators' of his time.

very positive steps to relieve indebtedness and to promote the use of credit for productive purposes. Many countries and regions have special Credit Co-operative Societies, to cater for the particular needs of their own peoples. The international Credit Union Movement is a linked system of credit co-operatives operating in many parts of the world.

PURE UNADULTERATED GOODS

In modern times with the numerous laws and regulations governing the sale of goods on matters of weights and measures, trade descriptions, fair trading, hygiene etc., this old Rochdale principle sounds archaic. It is no longer stated as a co-operative principle, but like the 'cash trading' concept it still lingers in the Co-operative philosophy in the context of quality goods and value for money. We often hear these sentiments expressed in such sayings as 'A poor man cannot afford a cheap coat' or 'the good article is the cheapest in the long run'. Many Co-op shops still favour quality goods and refuse to deal in shoddy articles and the rubbishy end of the market. They are cautious in regard to gimmicky products, suspected 'quack' remedies or any goods or services of doubtful value which may be advertised beyond their true capacity or intrinsic worth. The Co-operative Movement is opposed to the exploitation of the person, the community and the common people. It seeks to protect and enhance the quality of life at every level and resists anything that would diminish it, be it individual sharp practice or more widespread destruction of the physical or moral environment — the wilful waste or destruction of the earth's resources for financial gain or other supposed advantages. The Co-operative ethic also basically rejects such modern concepts as planned obsolescence and wasteful manufacturing or service techniques designed to promote the 'throw-away' and 'disposable' society.

Over the years also this Rochdale Principle has influenced co-operative thinking in a constructive reaction to these problems. Many older Co-ops carried the concept of dealing only in pure unadulterated goods to the point of not stocking items which were deemed to be less than conducive to the general health and wellbeing of their members e.g. alcohol, tobacco and in some cases even such things as hair-dyes and cosmetics! There has been a revival of this thinking in recent times. There are now some Co-operative Shops which by agreement of their members seek to guide peoples' attitudes and lifestyles in a helpful direction. They may continue to stock drink and cigarettes for the convenience of those who seek them but at prices *higher* than those obtaining elsewhere. On the other hand, they often offer considerable inducements, financial or otherwise, to promote the use of beneficial products and health foods. In America for example there are Co-operative General Stores which supply gardening implements and athletic gear at cost price or less to their members, where you can buy brown bread cheaper than white bread, whole rice cheaper than polished rice and so on. Some also, by the use of discounts, seek to guide their members towards better tastes in music, pictures, house decoration and furnishings. Thus by agreement they use their co-operative structure and a system of 'rewards and penalties' to promote the physical, social and cultural development of their members. At this point you may observe a co-operative practice inspired by one Rochdale Principle coming to merge with another.

EDUCATION IN CO-OPERATION

The Co-operative Movement has always laid stress on the need to educate its members. The Rochdale Pioneers and indeed the early pioneers of institutional co-operation in Ireland had to contend with the educational problem at a very basic level — many co-op members were illiterate and had little or no knowledge of the ways of business. It was extremely difficult in such circumstances to give members a real understanding of co-operative principles and co-operative ideals. People who live a long time in poverty and ignorance find it very hard to begin to believe that their lives can ever be really and permanently improved.

Today, although the cruder educational needs are somewhat better met, there is still a great need for education in Co-operation. In order to become committed and effective co-operators, members must learn a lot about Co-operation in all its different aspects. To learn the lessons of the past they need to know something of the history of the movement. They must have a grounding in co-operative 'principles' and practices, acquiring not only business expertise but also the organisational and social skills which help people to work together more efficiently and harmoniously. New knowledge and skills are always required as people come to apply the co-operative principle to new areas of human endeavour in a changing world.

POLITICAL AND RELIGIOUS NEUTRALITY

This guideline does not suggest that co-op members should give up the practice of religion or politics — the opposite would be nearer the truth. The Co-operative Movement encourages people to believe and live up to their beliefs. They are also urged as good citizens to play an active part in politics — the science and art of government — at neighbourhood, local and national level. There is a co-operative faith (embodying religion and politics) which asserts that the noblest aspiration of a man is to govern himself and to help devise, implement and support systems of good order and control in the community and the nation such as would permit and encourage the fullest development of the human person in his economic, social and cultural life.

Patrick Gallagher (1871-1966)

Paddy Gallagher, known as 'Paddy the Cope', was the great folk hero of the Irish Co-operative Movement ('cope' is a clipped northern abbreviation of the word 'co-operative'). A simple country boy with very little formal education, Gallagher first came into contact with the co-op idea in Scotland where he worked as a miner. Later he returned to his native district of the Rosses, Co. Donegal, where, in 1906, in the face of enormous difficulties and fierce opposition, he founded the famous Templecrone Co-operative Society. The story of his life is entertainingly told in his autobiography *My Story — Paddy the Cope.*

Not every co-operative association sets out to change the whole world or the whole social order overnight — indeed none of them do! They often set themselves a very limited objective in a very limited area — to get a better price for their produce, better pay for their work, cheaper goods or services, cheaper loans, better amenities. When their basic aim has been achieved they may expand their operation or tackle new activities. On the other hand, they may decide that with their limited resources and limited support they should more wisely continue to do one small job and do it well, content that their co-operative effort, albeit small, has a beneficial and moderating influence on private enterprise and public activity in that particular sector. This is legitimate and praiseworthy — the small co-op with its modest aims is changing its small bit of the world for the better. It retains its motivation in the knowledge that it is part of an overall movement which without being fanciful or over optimistic still has as its core aim a better social order — a New Moral World. This cannot be effected in practical terms in everyday life without a great deal of reference to people's political and religious activities, beliefs and aspirations.

Politics and religion are realities of life and cannot be ignored. What the Co-operative principle does enjoin is that the Co-operative association and its working organisation should not be manipulated or used to give unfair advantage to a particular political or religious group. The religious and political beliefs of all members should be respected but must not be allowed to become a divisive element within the co-operative. The object of the Co-operative Movement is to unite people rather than divide them. This co-operative principle is now regarded as implicit in the principle of open membership.

INTERNATIONAL CO-OPERATIVE PRINCIPLES

We have mentioned that the Rochdale Principles Nos. 5 and 6 concerning cash trading and dealing only in pure unadulterated goods are no longer explicitly named amongst the generally accepted list of modern co-operative 'guidelines'. Also, Principle 8 (Political and Religious neutrality) has now been incorporated with Principle No. 1 (Open membership). With a new and important guideline added this leaves us with a total of six International Co-operative Principles now accepted world-wide, and most recently endorsed at the Congress of the International Co-operative Alliance at Vienna in 1966. They are as follows:—

1. **Open Membership:** Membership of a co-operative society should be voluntary and available without artificial restriction or any social, political, racial or religious discrimination, to all persons who can make use of its services and are willing to accept the responsibilities of membership.

2. **Democratic Control:** Co-operative societies are democratic organisations. Their affairs should be administered by persons, elected or appointed, in a manner agreed by the members and accountable to them. Members of primary societies should enjoy equal rights in voting (one member, one vote) and participation in decisions affecting their societies. In other than primary societies, the administration should be conducted on a democratic basis in a suitable form.

3. **Limited Return on Share Capital:** Share capital should receive only a strictly limited rate of interest, if any.

4. **Disposal of Surplus:** Surplus or savings, if any, arising out of the operations of a society, belong to the members of that society and should be distributed in such a manner as would avoid one member gaining at the expense of others. This may be done by decision of the members as follows:

   (a) by provision for development of the business of the co-operative;

   (b) by provision of common service;

   (c) by distribution among the members in proportion to their transactions with the society.

5. **Education:** All co-operative societies should make provision for the education of their members, officers and employees and of the general public, in the principles and technique of co-operation, both economic and democratic.

6. **Co-ops Co-operate:** All Co-operative organisations, in order to best serve the interests of their members and the communities, should actively co-operate in every practical way with other co-operatives at local, national and international levels.

DIFFERENT TYPES OF CO-OPERATIVE

We have already seen something of the way in which a *Consumer Co-operative* works.

The basic pattern is the same in a great many consumer co-ops even though in external appearance they would appear to be very different from our simple Co-operative Shop where the members supplied themselves with groceries. In the broad sense we could apply the term *consumer co-operative* to any co-operative which deals in things that people *consume* or use — whether these be products or services. Even credit co-operatives come into the consumer category to the extent that their members seek to provide themselves with money on the best possible terms. Likewise, a society may seek to provide its members with housing, home-heating,

Robin Anderson (1860-1942)

Robert Andrew Anderson was a farmer's son, born near Buttevant, Co. Cork. He joined Horace Plunkett as co-op organiser in 1889. He travelled the length and breadth of Ireland by train, horse-trap and bicycle, organising co-operatives. In the early days his modest salary was paid by the Co-operative Union, Manchester. He was secretary of the IAOS (the organisational body for co-ops) from its foundation in 1894 until 1922, and president from 1933 until his death on Christmas Day, 1942. The IAOS was once described as an organisation of which 'Plunkett is the brains, Æ the spirit, and Anderson the energy'. He figures largely in all the records and his own book, *With Horace Plunkett in Ireland.* makes interesting reading.

electricity, telephones, roads, water supplies, television reception or babysitters, traffic wardens, home-helps or dustmen! Consumer co-ops as a general principle aim at supplying their members with goods and services at prime cost by availing of the cost reductions to be got by dealing in larger quantities and by reducing incidental costs through better organisation and business methods. Making your money buy more, though very important, is not the only reason for setting up co-ops. Many co-ops have consideration for the social, cultural and 'spiritual' economies as well. They think more in terms of 'total value satisfactions' and so do not necessarily concentrate all their efforts on the areas of the greatest and most immediate financial benefit.

Consumer Co-operation is the most important arm of the Co-operative Movement. Everybody is a consumer! It is only when the Co-operative Consumer base has been soundly established that the other branches of the movement can operate to full advantage and the whole Co-operative Movement becomes widespread and meaningful in the life of the people and of the nation.

PRODUCER CO-OPERATIVES

In a way you could say that the producer co-operative is the opposite of the consumer co-op. Consumers try to buy goods (or services) at the right price. The producer society on the other hand is a co-operative composed of people who come together and produce things and sell or dispose of their product(s) to best advantage. You will see the possibility of conflict here in the fact that the more money the producer gets for his product, the more the consumer has to pay for it. In the modern world, however, the primary producer and the ultimate consumer very rarely meet and deal directly with each other. They are often quite remote from each other both in the spatial (geographical) and the business sense so that between the producer and the consumer there may be many 'middle men' — the prime buyer who wholesales the raw goods to an exporter (transporter) who conveys them to a packer or processor (manufacturer) who sells in bulk to another wholesaler who sells to the retail shopkeepers before the goods get to their final destination.

This marketing process can be good or bad. It can be inefficient and costly if a middle man takes too much profit, if the transport or distribution systems are inadequate — or for other reasons.

In such a situation the *individual* producer and the individual consumer may feel quite helpless. The *producer co-operative* and the *consumer co-operative*, however, can often come a great deal of the way to meet each other and this can be of great advantage to their respective members.

They can cut out the middle man if they can do the job more efficiently themselves. There still remains the problem of resolving how this 'saving' is shared out i.e. what is a fair reward for the producer and a fair price to the consumer. This calls for clear understanding and a measure of goodwill. Again the important consideration is that 'fair play' is in the long-term interest of both parties — everyone is a consumer; and very often the *consumer* of one commodity is the *producer* of another. From the start, the pioneers of the Co-operative Movement were attracted by the ideal of a *Co-operative Commonwealth* — a system wherein producers and consumers would see the wisdom of treating each other fairly and where people as a community would have some control over their destiny by 'taking their business into their own hands'. Much hardship and human suffering could be avoided if people took an active part in determining how their business should be done, and if, in a controlling position, they *co-operated* with each other rather than aligning themselves in sectional interest groups to fight each other and exploit the weaker and less organised sections. Idealism apart, even the economist's theory of the 'free market' i.e. the free and sensible operation of market forces, supply and demand etc. cannot really operate where powerful individuals or groups are permitted to exploit the common people by manipulating markets, creating shortages or imposing artificial restraints on the supply or demand of goods, services or money.

HOW A PRODUCER CO-OPERATIVE WORKS

In Ireland the Co-operative Creamery is the most common example of a producer co-op. People often make the casual remark that 'farmers sell their milk to the creamery' and indeed to the outside observer, this is what appears to happen. In the case of a true co-operative the reality is quite different.

The farmers assemble their milk for manufacture and sale; each has contributed money by way of share capital and the co-op has obtained necessary loan capital -

To build factory (creamery) equipped with all the machinery and facilities to pack and process milk.

To employ workers and managers with special skills to manufacture and sell milk products, to keep accounts and generally manage and organise the business on efficient lines.

The farmer members own the business and continue to own the product(s) up to the point of sale.

The original milk may end up for sale in various forms to suit the market and to get the best return —

Bottled milk for human consumption, fresh or processed cream, cream liqueurs, butter, cheese, yoghurt, skim milk powder, baby foods, invalid formulae, milk replacers (animal feed) or other by-products for manufacturing industry e.g. casein for plastics.

All this is undertaken because raw milk is a very perishable product which will not remain fresh for more than a short period. All the milk that farmers produce cannot be sold for drinking. Individual farmers may not have the time or the means (organisation, skills, or money) to sell whole milk or to make and sell milk products such as butter and cheeses. People who produce perishable products have a very poor bargaining power on the market. If they do not sell immediately the product is lost — it cannot be taken home and kept until a better price can be obtained. Buyers were very aware of this and often offered very poor prices when there was a plentiful supply — the price also reflecting the risk *they* had to take. This is why farmers came together to form a co-operative society to preserve and manufacture their milk to ensure orderly marketing and a fair price.

In the dairy co-operative (creamery) money is received when the various milk products are sold.

From this we must deduct the cost of sales i.e. all the manufacturing costs and expenses which have been adding up since the members first brought their fresh milk to the creamery platform (intake point). These include wages and salaries, insurance, heat, light and power, depreciation and repairs on buildings and machinery, packaging, transport, telephones and postage, loan interest and bank charges, advertising, marketing and incidental expenses.

It is only when this has been done that we can establish the nett price that the farmer-members are realising for their milk.

Sales — Cost of Sales = value of raw milk.

This value figure divided by the total volume of milk assembled gives the average value of a unit volume (litre, gallon) of milk as taken into the creamery.

Of course the individual farmer-member cannot wait until the end of the accounting year to get money for his milk. He has to meet his own living expenses and the costs of running his farm. To do this he has to draw some money out of his co-operative on a regular basis somewhat in the same way as workers sometimes 'sub' on their wages i.e. drawing some money in advance before pay-day. In practice the farmer draws a great deal of his money in advance by way of monthly cheques from his co-operative. The monthly cheque is based on the volume (and quality) of milk which he has supplied to his factory at a 'price' per litre or per gallon estimated by the management to approximate quite closely to the final nett value. Not all the milk suppliers are rewarded at the same rate. Payment varies up and down on a scale designed to give each member a fair return for the quality of milk supplied. Milk with high butterfat and protein content gives better manufacturing return and so it is more highly *rewarded,* whilst there are price *penalties* to discourage the production and supply of milk which is below a certain standard.

The trading 'surplus' in a creamery co-op, therefore, (as in any producer co-op) arises as follows:

Sales of finished products minus Cost of Sales = Nett worth of these Products

Nett worth of Products minus Advance drawings by members = SURPLUS.

In big creamery co-ops, with several thousand member suppliers and a large milk supply, the end-of-year trading 'surplus' can be substantial even where the suppliers have already withdrawn sums only fractionally short of the true value of their milk. Where 'payment-on-account' for milk i.e. member withdrawals have been more cautious there may be a large surplus. Conversely, where the prepayments to the members are in excess of the true value of the milk there will be a trading deficit. Most co-ops try to leave sufficient margin in their prepayments to avoid this but it can sometimes arise due to unforeseen circumstances — market failure, drop in supply, unexpectedly heavy costs or faulty budgeting. This deficit will have to be made good, which means that the members will have to take a smaller return for their milk in the following season. When there is a 'surplus' the members of the society at the a.g.m. (annual general meeting) must decide how it is to be disposed. The options are:

(a) Surplus can be voted entirely to 'reserves' — to build up common capital for future developments etc.

(b) Total surplus distributed either in cash or shares to members in proportion to the quantity or value of milk each has supplied.

Cheese storage in a modern co-operative creamery.

(c) Part distributed — part to reserves, or part or all allocated to any other purpose by agreement of the members.

The surplus belongs to the members and they have absolute discretion within the law and the general rules of their society as to what they do with it. They may give it to charity or devote it to educational or other purposes, pay a 'bonus' to their employees or invest it in some other enterprise. They will of course have the advice of expert people, within their own ranks and from outside, as to what should be most profitably and prudently done, bearing in mind the immediate and long-term future of their co-operative.

MARKETING CO-OPERATIVES

In the past there was a tendency to have co-operatives which dealt only with a particular part or stage of the production or selling process. We had and still have co-ops which are involved only in selling primary unprocessed produce e.g. cattle and fish auction marts. Other co-ops concerned themselves only in organising such things as crop spraying or grain harvesting or, in the industrial sphere, doing just one part of the manufacturing process. Nowadays the trend is more towards an integrated approach. We no longer talk very much about *making* (producing) and *selling* but rather conceive of *marketing* as a process which covers every aspect of the total activity from the time the first stages of production are planned until the final product reaches the consumer. For example creamery co-ops nowadays are not content to accept milk as they find it on the intake platform but do an important job with their supplies - their members 'inside the farm gate' planning the profitable production of more and better milk as well as guiding the farmer in other enterprises being undertaken on his farm. At the other end of the scale the creamery of course is very concerned about the sale of the finished dairy products.

SPECIALISED MARKETING

It is not possible to draw rigid lines to distinguish between what is strictly a production co-operative and a marketing co-operative. However, when the *primary* co-op (i.e. the co-op composed of individual primary producers) has done its best there may still be need for a specialised service in final marketing. Marketing Co-operatives are often *secondary* co-ops as distinct from *primary* co-ops. A secondary co-op, (it is more commonly called a federation) is really a co-op of co-ops i.e. the membership is not composed of individuals but of corporate co-operative societies. In the marketing area these federations have emerged because the primary co-ops find that there are added advantages to be gained by selling their products collectively. For the same or lesser marketing costs they find that by coming together they can afford to apply more expertise to the job of marketing — more regular deliveries, better promotion and advertising and all the sophisticated techniques which hopefully sell more products, leave better profits, satisfy more customers and ensure the longterm success of the producers' enterprise. Modern marketing involves much more than dealing, bargaining or even advertising. A very important part of it involves keeping in touch with every area of the production process, feeding market information back down the lines so that the processors and the primary producers can plan and organise their production, perfect their own techniques and 'tailor' (adapt) their products to what the market demands. Bord Bainne is a secondary co-op. It markets practically all the dairy produce made by creamery co-ops in the Republic.

In producer co-operation the specialised Marketing Co-ops can be looked on as *wholesalers* — just as we have federations of co-op shops forming Wholesale Co-ops at the Consumer end.

LABOUR CO-OPERATIVES

The phrase 'labour co-operative' is not in common use but we introduce it here to illustrate more easily a distinction between basic co-op types and to trace what is often a tangled thread in the co-op fabric. We use the term here to distinguish people who co-operate to *maximise the value of their labour.* In the more basic form a labour co-operative is a business which does not have any assets or employ any capital but where the members pool their labour and skills in order to get the best return for them, usually by providing a service for others. A common example would be a number of workers and tradesmen who come together to build a house for another party where all the material and building requirements are provided by that party — in other words the workers are supplying nothing but their labour.

The workers form themselves into a registered co-operative Society. This gives them legal standing and certain benefits such as limited liability. Limited liability means that in the case of failure the members are not legally responsible for the total debts of their society but only for the amount of their own share capital. Unless they opt for other arrangements, all Co-operatives of every kind, registered under the Industrial and Provident Societies Acts are given the benefit of limited liability. This also applies to private companies registered under the Companies Acts. An extreme illustration — a company or co-operative, consisting only of seven members with a share capital of £1 each, fails in business and goes into liquidation. After all assets have been accounted for there is still £1,000,000 owing to creditors. Under the limited liability clause the shareholders are not *legally* required to shoulder the burden of this £1 million debt — they lose only £1 each. *Moral* responsibility is, of course, another matter. In practice, of course, it would be extremely difficult for a company with only £7 share capital to get such an amount of money to set up and run a business that could fail to the tune of £1 million. Lending agencies seek guarantees and security for loans to the greatest extent possible but it is common enough for businesses to fail owing up to ten times the amount of the owners' investment.

But to get back to our example of our, say seven worker-tradesmen planning to build a house. Having registered their co-operative — possibly with nominal share capital — the working procedures go something like this:

1. A contract is negotiated with the eventual houseowner fixing a total sum to be paid for the building work with arrangement for staged payments as the work proceeds.

2. Arrangements are made with a bank, credit union or other source for some loan capital.

3. The worker members agree to draw a given sum at regular intervals for living expenses. The usual arrangement is for each to draw every week a sum corresponding to what would be the ordinary week's wages, appropriate to his skill, if working for an employer.

4. A leader is appointed to organise the work, to keep the accounts and seek further contracts etc. Ideally all the members will be aware and alert and help out as required.

5. When the job is completed the situation will be reviewed. Depending on the time span, they may proceed with further contracts but at a suitable point they will hold a formal general meeting.

6. At the general meeting a full account will be given of the progress to date together with detailed financial returns.

Example:	£
Value of work done	10,000
less Fees, incidental expenses etc.	600
	9,400
less members' drawings	8,000
'Surplus'	1,400

The members must now decide what to do with the surplus.

Omagh Credit Union — typical of the 470 modern credit union offices in towns and villages throughout Ireland. The credit unions have over seven thousand members altogether and over £3 hundred million in savings.

(1) A common decision in such cases is to vote the entire surplus to 'reserves' against the day when the society will have enough money to buy materials and build houses for sale.

(2) The surplus may be distributed amongst the members in the form of additional shares. This also retains the money in the society.

(3) The members may have personal or family business requirements to be met which are deemed more pressing or more profitable for the time being than the capitalisation of their society. Accordingly, they may agree to distribute the surplus in cash.

(4) They may decide to distribute part of the surplus in cash and/or some in shares and vote the remainder to reserves.

When the surplus is distributed either in shares or in cash the allocation should be an equitable one. It is up to the members to agree on what is the fairest way. A common method is to divide the surplus between members in proportion to 'wages earned' i.e. the total hours worked multiplied by the normal hourly wage rate for that particular skill or grade paid in private enterprise (usually Trade Union rate). This is done on the basis of agreement that the more skilled workers have the more difficult, exacting and demanding work to do, bear more responsibility for the standard of the finished work and so contribute more to the Surplus. However, a proportionately higher share of the surplus on top of already higher 'drawings' (on a differential rate) may create a big gap between the total rewards of different workers. If this is felt to be undesirable the members may agree on any one of a number of different methods e.g. they may decide on a straight-forward distribution to each worker on the basis of 'hours worked' regardless of skill or grade or they may distribute part on a flat hourly rate and the remainder on a differential scale.

Co-operatives of every kind are conscious of basic tenets of social equity; and there is a philosophical leaning towards the concept of equalisation of rewards. This is based on the belief that only to a very limited extent, if any, is any trade, profession or occupation to be deemed 'superior' to any other. We have the ideal concept of the co-op being a 'family' and in this context many early co-operative communes tried to operate a system whereby each member 'contributed to the best of his ability and was supported (rewarded) in accordance to his needs'. It may sound rather utopian in the ambience of capitalist business but it is yet the principle which is successfully operated within the ordinary domestic scene in families and kinship groups. 'Labour' co-operatives are particularly sensitive on the matter of differential rewards and many consider it undesirable even in large co-operatives to have a differential of more than 3 or 4 to 1 between the pay of the chief executive and that of the most newly-arrived recruit.

In some countries there are examples of co-operatives which try to retain an undiluted identity as 'labour co-operatives' seeking only to provide work opportunities and/or maximise the value of their members' labour. Often they have very little share capital and own little or no assets. They rent their requirements of buildings, machinery and equipment and 'hire' working capital through a system of personal guarantees or other arrangements from some lending agency — frequently from an associated co-operative bank or credit society. This approach arises from the ideological belief, which is a reversal of the capitalist norm, that Labour should employ Capital rather than Capital employ Labour.

In practice it is exceedingly difficult to maintain a co-operative situation in which the 'labour' component is the total focus of the co-operative effort.

As our primitive co-op of seven building workers makes progress there is usually a build-up of share capital and capital assets — building materials, houses, machinery and equipment. Membership grows and the business diversifies so that in due course it becomes a Producer Co-operative selling a product or products to other people. This is very similar to the situation which applies in the case of our farmers producing, processing and selling milk where the farmers are seeking the best rewards available for products which arise because of the use of not one but a number of resources:

(1) their own and their hired labour

(2) their personally owned assets — farmlands, stock, buildings, equipment and cash

(3) their collectively owned assets — factory buildings, equipment etc.

In other words the members of a Producer Co-operative seek a return not only on their Labour but also on their Investment.

WORKER OWNERSHIP IN INDUSTRY

In recent times there is increasing interest in the idea of workers owning the business in which they work. Even capitalist private enterprise is concerned to find suitable systems of 'worker participation'. It is generally accepted that if workers have a stake in the business a lot of industrial troubles are lessened if not entirely cured — absenteeism, low productivity, strikes, etc.

The degree of worker participation in industry varies over a wide range from a small shareholding and a consultative contact with management, to total worker ownership and management control.

The worker-owned worker-managed Productive Society or 'labour'co-operative is most often found in manufacturing industry especially in the light engineering and craft sectors but there are successful self-managed workers' co-operatives in a great many different enterprises in service industry. The Mondragon co-operative development enterprises in northern Spain are all based on the concept of common ownership.

Common ownership workers co-ops often have certain distinctive features:

- The capital assets of the co-operative are vested in a Trust and so cannot be sold by the workers and the proceeds divided for individual financial gain.

- Although many people may be shareholders and members of the society, only the *workers* have voting rights, or any say in the management of the business.

- The individual workers take a very substantial shareholding in the business from the start. Far from thinking that the world owes them a living or the entitlement to a job, they are prepared to put up the capital necessary to provide employment. This is often of the order of half a year's wages or more, some of which is paid up immediately and which is added to by regular payments in much the same way as a hired worker in private capitalist enterprise arranges deductions from his wages.

- There is usually a probationary period before the worker is admitted to full membership — usually 6 months to one year. In this time both the applicant (who is as yet only hired and paid a weekly wage) and the existing members will have a chance to assess each other. The applicant's suitability for full membership will be judged on his ability to live and work in harmony with his fellow workers, his working skills and his enthusiasm for the idea as reflected in such matters as his record in saving for his share-capital investment.

- The rules usually lay down that a sizeable percentage of the 'surplus' must be voted to reserves or for development purposes.

- A limit is often set to the extent to which 'hired labour' may be employed.

- Industrial common ownership enterprises often work in close accord with co-operative credit societies, Credit Unions or other co-operative or State sources of finance geared to their special needs.

CO-OPS IN PRACTICE

We have introduced the terms 'producer', 'consumer' and 'labour' merely to illustrate particular aspects of co-operative endeavour. Co-operation is a pervasive movement and in the multifaceted business of human living the analyst cannot hope to draw clear distinctions thinking that his rigid lines will remain intact. Life is *organic* in that everything relates in some way to everything else and it is *dynamic* in that it is always moving and changing.

The wider ambition of the Co-operative Movement is to encompass all aspects of human living, applying *the co-operative principle* that people should everywhere work together for their individual and common benefit. People are consumers of many things and producers of some — nearly all are workers in some sense. Consequently we find in practice many co-operatives which contain elements of more than one of the crude basic 'co-op types' we have tried to describe. Name tags like 'producer' or 'consumer' may be useful in describing enterprises at the "start-up" stage but it is not good to see them retained by developed co-operatives. Indeed, if a co-operative retains a clearly defined identity as a 'producer' or 'consumer' co-op one is fearful of the extent of *selfishness,* rather than true *co-operation,* in the venture.

The larger multipurpose type of co-operative, for example a Farmer Co-operative, may include under one structure several different types of production and consumer co-operation closely inter-related to each other, and to a 'labour' co-operation also, depending on how the hired workers are involved and how they are rewarded. Some services operated by Farmer Co-operatives are almost self-contained "co-operative labour" ventures e.g. relief milking teams, farm machinery and farm building work squads.

Simple Model of a Business

THE FIRM

Production
and/or
distribution

Capital   Labour   Raw Materials   Consumers

The kind of name-tag we put on the firm depends to a great extent on who does what!

If the *suppliers of labour* hire capital, buy raw materials and sell to consumers and take the 'margin' as a profit (return on their capital) we have something like a *Workers' Co-operative* or a *self managed family*

If the *suppliers of capital* hire labour, buy raw materials and sell to consumers and accept a residual variable reward for their own labour we have something like a *Workers Co-operative* or a *self managed family firm* or a *professional partnership* e.g. engineers, accountants.

If the *suppliers of raw materials* hire capital and labour at contractual rates, sell to consumers and accept a residual (variable) return on their raw materials we have something like a simple form of *producers' co-op.*

Where the *Consumers* hire capital, hire labour, buy materials and accept the surplus/deficit as a variable price for the final product we have something akin to a *Consumer co-operative.*

As we have already said, simple models such as these are comparatively rare. In the real world of working Co-operatives, you often find very complex arrangements. A co-op may have equity, share capital and borrowed capital — labour co-ops may hire other labour, producers' co-ops buy in raw materials from non-members and consumer co-ops sell to non-members at fixed prices.

Also we have the complexity arising from combinations of activities as in the previously mentioned example of a Farmers' Co-operative. Many creamery societies in Ireland process their members' milk, procure most of their farm inputs (seeds, fertilisers) and take in other produce of members such as grain, the processed output of which goes as an input to other members viz. animal feed. A single co-op may be engaged in all these and several other activities in the way of 'consumer' services to its members.

BOOKS TO READ

Briscoe et al, *The Co-operative Idea* (Cork, Bank of Ireland Centre for Co-op Studies) 1982

M. Linehan, C. O'Leary, V. Tucker, *How to Start a Co-op* (Cork, Bank of Ireland Centre for Co-op Studies) 1981

M. Linehan & V. Tucker, *Workers' Co-operatives* (Cork, Bank of Ireland Centre for Co-op Studies) 1983

Patrick Bolger, *The Irish Co-operative Movement* (Dublin, Institute of Public Administration) 1977

Arnold Bonner, *British Co-operation* (Manchester, Co-operative Union) 1970

R. A. Anderson, *With Horace Plunkett in Ireland* (London, Macmillan) 1935

M. Digby, *Horace Plunkett: An Anglo-American Irishman* (Oxford, Basil Blackwell) 1949

Horace Plunkett, *Ireland in the New Century* (reprint Dublin, Irish Academic Press) 1982

G. W. Russell, *Co-operation and Nationality* (reprint Dublin, Irish Academic Press) 1982

R. O'Connor & P. Kelly, *A Study of Industrial Workers' Co-operatives* (Dublin, Economic and Social Research Institute) 1980

E. T. Craig, *An Irish Commune: History of Ralahine* (reprint Dublin, Irish Academic Press) 1983

Patrick Gallagher, *My Story — Paddy the Cope* (Dungloe, Templecrone Co-op Society) n.d.